OTHER BOOKS BY MICHAEL GIZZI

My Grandfather's Pants, Bench Press (1973)
Carmela Bianca, Bonewhistle Press (1974)
Bird As, Burning Deck (1976)
Avis, Burning Deck (1979)
Species of Intoxication, Burning Deck (1983)
Just Like a Real Italian Kid, The Figures (1990)
Continental Harmony, Roof Books (1991)
gyptian in hortulus, Paradigm Press (1991)
Interferon, The Figures (1995)

NO BOTH

Michael Gizzi

*For Suzanne
Best wishes
Michael Gizzi*

*Lenox
26 x 97*

Hard Press/The Figures
1997

Cover collage, *No Both* (1994) 5 1/6" x 6 3/4" by Barbieo Barros-Gizzi.

Grateful acknowledgment to the editors of the periodicals in which many of these poems first appeared: *Prosodia, Object, Provincetown Arts, lingo, Agni, Mirage/Periodical, The World, o.blek, Triangle Shirtwaist Fire, Lift, First Intensity, Avec, Sulfur, Hotbird Mfg., Bughouse, Rhizome, New American Writing* and *The Gertrude Stein Awards in Innovative Writing 1994-95*; in *That Various Field for James Schuyler,* edited by William Corbett and Geoffrey Young, The Figures, 1991; *Under One Roof,* edited by Barry Sternlieb, Mad River Press, 1992; *The Poet's Calendar for the Millenium,* Sun & Moon, 1997.

Versions of some of these poems appeared in the chapbook *Interferon,* The Figures, 1995. "The Rejected Perfume" appeared in *Rejection,* The Figures, 1997. Thanks to Trevor Winkfield for providing several titles and to Geoffrey Young for invaluable editiorial assistance. "Louis Thunder Gallstone Death" derives from a Jack Kerouac radio interview with Charles Jarvis and James Curtis, WCAP, Lowell, 1962.

Copyright © 1997 by Michael Gizzi
ISBN: 1889097-160

Published in the United States by The Figures & Hard Press, Inc, a non-profit organization: P.O. Box 184, West Stockbridge, MA 01266

Gizzi, Michael
   No both / Michael Gizzi.
   p. cm. (Lingo series)
   ISBN 1889097-160
   I. Title II. Series: Lingo series (Hard Press)
   PS3557.I9 N6 1997
   811/.54 21   97-038286
                                                  CIP

*for my brothers
Tom and Pete*

TABLE OF CONTENTS

I. NO BOTH

"Only last night because I'm always" 13
"Dear Bushwhack Saint Tacky of Bombazine" 15
"Christ clocked at a buck-ten on I-91" 16
"Ripley" 17
"A few times in our lives we live like cats" 18
"A mind to halfmoon a lunatic" 19
"With vexation" 20
"Get your ass outta my soul" 21
"Then went about on little ant knees" 22
"A bald narcissist" 23
"Nostalgia is an impossible language" 24
"Sunup in the kitchen corner" 25
"Mr Bing Crosberry" 26
"I built this rear window" 27
"Summer affected her dolphin" 28
"Gawking under the influence" 29
"The sun won't stay blind" 30
"The Miracle of the Growing Macaroni" 31
"This is only the sixth time" 32
"A near myth childhood hovercraft" 33
"A case of life" 34
"A sermon precipitant of runoff" 35
"The only remnant of a yen I'll get" 36
"Wanton troopers gliding by" 37
"When I die which I weather will be soon" 38
"A day to duck under" 39
"500 mikes of windowpane" 40
"I shop at the Noble Savage store" 41
"O hymen! O criminy!" 42

"Thank the Mighty Clouds of Joy" 43
"Who has fame in mind will defame his kind" .44
"Signal smoke curling like woodsmoke" 45
"When your eyes have room I visit" 46
"Suppose we yawned" 47
"Say listen Uncle Son" 48
"A doll is playing with the minutes" 49
"Strings shoot out of the ground" 50
"One Trick Tony weepy in rooster chaps" .51
"Wanting life" 52
"Louis Thunder Gallstone Death" 53
"Non-union trees tossing noggin-topped Nijinskis" 54
"In intravenous spring" 55
"The hand that spreads" 56
"Stewnauts collect old teapots" 57
"Planets around the mainstem" 59
"Think of guys high in front of espresso machines" 60
"I've been sick all my life" 61

II. WE SEE

Bird on Dial 65
A Brodeyak 67
Dante Enters Tibet 68
In the Vicinity of a Grocer 69
Too Big Canader 71
In Memory of Brazilla Ray 74
Piltdown Audibles 75
They Say It's Wonderful 76
The Incumbents in Her Garden 77
North of the Sunset 80
Code of Silence 84
Tripoli 85

Independence Eve	86
Joujouka Anaesthetist	88
Parker's Point, Chester	91
Tristano Solo	93
The Golden Book of Resentment	94
For Carla in Frisco a Listener	95
Ask Me Now	97
The Permanence of Whim to Providence	98
When Goodies Start to Fail	99
Mornithology	101
McKenna's All Saints	103
Exoduster	104
The Rejected Perfume	106
Ma Predicate	108
Newk's Time	109
To a Dutch Astronomer in the Netherlands	110
Ode to Woody Strode	111
The Academy of False Hope	114
Lompoc in Spring	115

No
Both

> "I pity the poor immigrant
> Who wishes he would've stayed home."
> *Bob Dylan*

> "That's life."
> *Frank Sinatra*

Only last night because I'm always growing a proboscis I said "Tomorrow I'll begin this new notebook with the words *I surrender.*" Like I should have a scarlet brand on my lip in lieu of a moustache that reads "He begins on the morrow" or tattooed to my big toe "He died with his rue on." But even that's a scarlet ruse. No wonder I suffer such trapezoidal travel anxiety that to put it wildly I get this visual visceral hallucination that my chest extends six feet straight out like an amphetamine puffed mourning dove. Might have something to do with flight. What's that, Doctor Pancoat, my little fraidy cat flights from change?

I always have a sense of camaraderie whenever I hear women especially remark quite rightly "Men? —yes, they're terrified of change." And yet if I'm going to make a clean stab at the brisket of it *the truth* best be careful not to piss off the mark and traffic only in a bloodbath of my own shirttail shortcomings trailing a Roman nosebleed—them I know exceedingly well. After all I'm not the Desquamated Professor of Grey Torpor for nothing.

But I desire a chair not a pitypot in perpetuity. I want a palpable hit. But I regress. I'm back kneeling on bitter rice in the coldstone circus church of misbehaving bent youth, slurring three-square Marys, faking a good Act of Conniption flush in front of the Light-a-Candle Concession, a terraced altar of carmine-colored jellyglasses flickering their translucent booboos of Jesus. Tongues of fire for hire? Drop the geetus in the leadbox and indulge your poor dead Pop with a night on the town in Limbo. A plaque on your house! Sister Tetchy scoring my penance ringside humphing siroccos through the bat wings on her Shroud of Turin.

"A beating a day keeps the titters away" peel the Bells of Saint Scary. Hang it all, Buster Brown, but we attended a condemned school. No wonder everyone I see points the fingers in their faces at me. Some can't accept a little hotsoup kitchen less it's been divined by their own dowsers, whence this Christer's scupper of cripes. You can imagine where this manic ringworm road goes. Flatline seems to be status quo and yet if you're a frantic mountaineer-like Mindanao diver you quiver wishbone in scabbard a being so bi-polar you either consign yourself to the blasted blame-box or turn your entirely flayed caul of pain on the world's largesse.

You know what the guy who ate the school said to me? "I thought it was Prince of Gluttony Day." A telltale sign of instability responsible for many memorable events. Why can't one have fun in his/her own home? But in our misty roses we forget.

Dear Bushwhack Saint Tacky of Bombazine:

    I'm well aware I haven't yet surrendered but I can't keep my eye-fix inners off those severed breasts of Catherine (erect) on a platter. How can you request anyone surrender to a subsect inquisition of *humilitas* such as you expect? Life is a queer little man to quote Barry Fitzgerald but I'm not sure I want to bunk with him.

    It is the corning of the reign of ham. The eyes of knickers are upon us to be sung. Even the old fogies of Continuing Ed slip back into their saddle shoes after a Hindu session with thought balloons—the said sad unzipped blindstiff bifurcating the curb as Jimmy said "Once he was a little boy and his folks provided for him."

    Let it be spit on the sod's soiled neck with throat chimes: I may not like me but share my contact gardenhose of glee and no Richelieu of hypocrisy can stanch it.

P.S. Take a powder, Brother McFlea

Christ clocked at a buck-ten on I-91, fifteen pounds of pancake minkup. A contact bum of valorous stick-to-it-iveness sharp as Billy Occam's scar collection. Let's grow up and go to sleep, count seagulls saying kaddish over a lost harpoon. Wait a minute! wasn't I going somewhere? Although we speak a lost speech which ain't quite is it true and dive into the blind plural pastime like coins on Oedipus-eyes or Mister Sainted Mother Tough Tomato deaf as a hundred years, how is it knowledge gets lost and the meaning clear?

What a fella needs is mother-wit and a horsehair, or just another drubbing from his monkey Uncle Wrench. Daylights phrase our staggering stars. The sorrow of wild oats is to sodomize flies? Pull the rug out from under your road, there's a pothole promiscuous moon. I smell something locked-up *a cappella* saboteur.

11:00 to 3:00 is four hours and I think I slept for three which is a record for undisturbed me. I knew if I didn't slow down I'd be breaking bread on my father's knee in the bleep hereafter, blue as the sky left in the dark in a blind rage chilling a red face white, as when life bends your wrists back and the hearts on your sleeves fray.

Ripley,

Believe it or not but I just purchased my first rubber of rainskins at age 43 and brought 'em home kerplop in top drawer sock salter which I keep opening so's to peek see my father there in safety in my bedroom as I never was sneaking around in his. But condoms father nothing good or bad—sorry Reverend Mother Martyr "la Favorita."

The last time (one of them) together at the Audubon Sistine Bird Sanctuary arguing per usual that was our fun as though we'd straddle that high tension wire forever, neither of us giving in that was one definition of love and not a bad one because there's only the one life which we both knew but which most people fashimmeled forget.

He was standing in a mizzle in front of the talking parrot toucan what-do-you-call-it mynah bird cage, a nosehair stark sticking out in the air that only grey can illumine and I so athletic-like stepped up as if to slug a homerun which I'd done so many times before and which he'd refused to come see me do due to the high tension wire and with one swift swiping mongoose move I d'Artagnaned that hair right out of his nose. It was a tender moment especially for him as his eyes watered with pluck-pain and I knew in that photo-finishing moment I'd beat him by a hair which is also why his eyes watered with deadly sin of expression—the father and the son who finally subdues him.

And then the lecture scientific of course about the dangers of causing an aneurysm to the brain due to such daring pluck—a Scientific American death in front of a birdhut? I could fill a shoebox with nosehairs of foiled death-defying self-destructive feints at reunion. Between thumb and forefinger I tweeze another nosehair and whisper "Hang on, maybe this time I'm comin', Pop!"

A few times in our lives we live like cats
The child in us loves the applause
Watching is nothing
Angels are people who never blinked
I've seen them sniffing
I can see through you into the garage beyond
One day you'll sit in the sun and be incinerated
Sometimes terrible things happen quite naturally
I get up in the morning and there's my skin in bed
They got my head can you beat that
Then a wasp stung out my eye
Makes my hungry fist feel like the angel of mercy's compote
Skin shiny like a mirror seas of boiled fish
Ink like you've never seen
My sweat in a bottle dripping gasoline
The wind in the willies

A mind to halfmoon a lunatic
Send sunshine the shakes
Make hay hit the sack pinstripes
Rorschach equal parts
Potato hat with smoker's hack

Foot tubesocks on a cricket painter
Who hires a mermaid to clean his rock
Fasten victory bonnet with Ojibway gardenhose
Build pocket knives for townies
In the poems of Basho

Offend everyone I know
And have them thank me
Aren't I the wild eagle's bird tongue
Waxing the roof of his home widdershins?
A bug just took a picture of the sun

Some old artesian revelation of kin
Like the one leaf maple lone
Hung-on red through winter quorums
On which is being recorded now
The demo of spring's first birdsong

With vexation
On automatic self *sieg heil*
A little bird

Is throwing voices
Pick up your eyes
See as others see

Eureka feels like home
Grass stains on the sky
The hawk inside

Hello, Darling!
You sure is a sharpie
Beautifying the bee

Get your ass outta my soul you pastina-brained organdy
 wraith-maker.
Through this portal pass catapults befitting into a fist.
Gee wig! as far back as home is tomatoes cure the clap?
What am I buck-rebelling against?
Crickets!
Moreover, you're the torso contadina volunteer bridie
 freckle-tipped a pair of paint shoulderpants fell off
 some midget element like a fullsize twin.
Who was it Piero della Francesca'd your cinderblocks of
 misperspective?
You gonna blame that on cousin Ninganing too?
How could such beauty align itself with a drainpipe and
 stay there snaked?
Your dress like your home cantilevered in a prom date
 photo pic 1941, sixteen years before your first Olds
 Italiano statement of status quo arriviste nouveau
 leech creeping assimilation.
You dis-mug me.
I wanna barf on the beauty that *was* the foliage surrounding
 you in that '41 photo-op coppiced now like you and
 your tomato paste, all because I hate what they done to
 you and you let them do shutting me down like some
 Cinecitta ragazzi who died before he was born, my sick
 socked soul outworn bumming that Appian Way of all
 kids who want a break from Mama not just spaghetti.

Then went about on little ant knees a beetle shining back saying "Step on me." Now I'm beating myself with a liquid. Blackout Hamlet's debentures in the binge trade. Methinks do-dah Beauregard. Reading the world it appears everyone thinks they have an ear, but "You no got ear" unless you've found that lost ear of Van Gogh buried rotten like some queer cob of corn under earth in yellow Provence. Harvest uppers? The autistic slur of quiz kids. Poetry and waistcoats.

So language is a plot to make us think we're God's dogs and go sick 'em. Who said it's raining fish to the trees? My heart's so all fired up it's beating on the other side now. That level at which poetry is a compensation for a lack of conversation between any two of which we make much, like those guys who could go to the edge but go back inside to do some ice fishing instead. Closer I ever got to brothers, almost like my nose. The capguns of my enormous liberties. Mayakovsky in my backpocket headfirst.

Because I knew you wouldn't have a coffee without a smoke I saved this nail. Met an old dovetail in the sleet today. A Sycorax of mooncalves, I bite this War Between the States bullet, rats racing up and down inside my legs. The seat of my pants shiny like a nursery rhyme. The citizeneer down on his luck. And who invented the screw? I'd like to know all about it backwards. By George, ain't that Bigtop on pickup sticks?

O ye of little teeth, your cough that resembles the missing pounds of an old man.

A bald narcissist
is a hairless Greek Tragedy
an herbal phantom
in a glassy prison

Symbolism's
rocks in your head
broken-field run-
ning to Lapland

It is the business of the future
to be absent come back
and leave me
alone

Better than the cheekbones
on a classic telepathic
listening
to every photograph's word

Nostalgia is an impossible language attached to a dream casual as dirt. Visions caress a ramp called an error in Corinthians. Starlight, another ad for the sea. On the high seas (three of them flat) leaves move to reflect a monstrous endowment. A leaf in the magical plenitude of a nap speckles its branches.

The pensive memory of furious mettle and the tendons of a bird with two bills brilliant in the disposal my life reflects as a crystal shines on a diamond in feverish pain, and the smoking dogs in their venting degrees.

Now I enter the sea perpetual semblance of a quiet man smoking his fingers in an English pavilion. A dead guide we can chat with. The air of my heart arranges a race of knives. Truth may never enter the mind of what originally thought it.

after Jean Frémon

Sunup in the kitchen corner hands you back your head
    Odd to think the best's already dead
Sepulchral past-tense of the outside world loving its shell
    Sure a little childish thought of death felt irreversible
You thought if you could bury yourself you could manage without
    Even wicker understood at that moment you'd been dismissed

Dismissed I must tell you as long as I have been I am again
    That you should want me a has-been fallen open on the floor
On the floor something your tempo must be cruising for
    Will your neck be the private drawing I keep of you
When I am broken layed up as angels are across the sun
    Smells of faith on those days you smell like a gun

Mr Bing Crosberry Earl of Morning Birds is toting on his foolscap of cheek-sucking kerplunk an alphabet of every sun was ever sunup in his bailiwick, bicycle-pumping some buttermilk into the Pillsbury Doze Boys as though every morning the Navy reapplied for a Mayflower.

Achtunged awake at 4:18 a.m. Mr Terrapin now minus his carapace cares more than he thought possible in his shell-life, suddenly he has a Nagasaki on his chest, his turtleneck a soupy shade of green per Looney Tune cartoon zipping about shall we say with Robert Johnson in his Terraplane beating on every rabbitry door.

    "Hey Bunny you wanna play Pregnancy Test? You want a racy me?"

Go back to Queequeg you shrunken kingpin, you're a Jonah and that's why Goddy swallowed you like a star.

I'm gonna make some new skin
like being all at sea
It may be raining rugs in Spain
but in my pants it's raining ropes
There is no shame in Poetry

A bigmouth quiet as a dormouse

I built this rear window
    To hear my intensity
April's hem giving way to mayhem
    Some kind of Cochise misdirection?

I remember being the first
    To spit a 100 mph. Awful
Visceral the way the rush
    Drew my bicuspids

What might've made a tent-going man
    Bleed pesticides
Think I'll accentuate the retentive
    If you don't mind

Memory is addiction's divinity
    A treasure of Sierra
Measure border climes
    Old Slang Sid in songnets

This must be love illiterate
    Or aren't it when I get
That Lincoln stirrup songster
    Right between my eary eyes?

Ever smoke a canary?
    I make a beeline
For the birdcall
    Discarding an entire set of bones

Summer affected her dolphin
The tug of bait might've been a loved one
I thought of telephoning an animal
Of committing a lewd bottle-nosed annoyance
Graffito scrawled over sound of dripping in the wind
We wept into the beer pumps
Choice little grunts of the 5th largest tourist in these parts
Apart from the pie factory
The only work *is* painting

Our coats wished us well
There was a sign saying vacancies but that seemed nervous
Mind-readers make yourselves at home
There was a rose over the harbor in the distance
The mouth of the river struck by a propeller
Suffered eleven fins
The lifeboat agreed to behave in the water
Wave if you're in trouble
We wouldn't want the cold creeps over one

A touch was in the *wasser* caressing symmetry
The boat had trapped part of my laugh
You get all types grinned the world
A lady-in-waiting wanted to see a miracle
We'd prefer not to speak about our feelings
Read the visitor's book
Flamingoland confirmed the salmon sense
Newfangled disposal lads wanted to keep the sink
A shame about the wild sea

Gawking under the influence
   liquid elastic or look straight atcha
      Lolita-like topaz askance, one
O blood flaw fleur-de-lis in the yolk
   of her bel occhio
      hip-cresting Skybar in blur
               pingpong ball high on the breezeway

    Such a sultry smoking sash of sighs she don't even see it, do I? All those eunuchs beating around the bush deconstructing Orientalism, blowing blue cigarettes instead of teaching Flaubert's *The Incontinence*. Who isn't a shiny pants pervert in the privacy of his own headroom? Like a night in old movies out West cancan saloons, every time she takes a spill the talk of the town sure seems preoccupied with his lips.

    Like the one eye on a long Egyptian onion stalk I always swept the cheerleaders with, smooth volutes of thigh out of pleated shortskirt so much like sexy footbals in my iddy dirty mind on 50 yardline mid-stride of stroke, the Egyptian onion spyscope snaking beneath bleachers over cola cup crushed specimens of effervescent pearls on the inside chew-wax. Me heapbig hero-self jet-propelled by marching band scoring with pigskin, meaning meanwhile this'll bring 'em to their feet standing in the stands so's I can peer up Eileen Lulu and Sue which is a mortal sin. By God I hope so! I had a bellyfull of backlots, an aria-hole in my head, on my helmet a Latin crib for the deep safety—'cause I'm goin' deep!

The sun won't stay blind
Sine waves now have a harem

Like a tarpaulin we expect them to rustle an angel
Footsore on the rubber floor of the bird room

What this has to do with schizophrenic
Shrunken heads strapped to chair legs

Vivaldi declining the syringe odd weekends
Visionary tins of petticoat hunting barbs

Suits cut to hide other men

She'd like a sleep so foreign floor-to-ceiling
Driftwood parrots sounding Mayan

No one would know at that moment
How tough it is to be cotton

By the side of the road calming tents

The Miracle of the Growing Macaroni like Jesus and the Little Fishes. Marconi cajoling the 2nd class coming of fazool. Like Noonoo and Nonnie pastina blimps of respectable poverty reading aloud from pats of butter.

Noonoo—the John Henry jackhammer self-conscious paesan of little Maria Rilkean spiritual work veils—practicing veronicas in the wardrobe they won't accept in the other world, who wore behind his ear sawdust every night that his wife might enjoy the smell of wood.

If I knew him (I did in infancy) when I dreamed I was convinced I knew him (Viareggio stories bounce me on his knee like a rosso rubber sfero) but he was bald by then no longer that Red Italian like Red Malcolm X which distinguished them both but somehow all coalesced in that *Red Balloon* French children's book for American kids wherein I confused or clarified it sussing out a little European boyhood picturesque—me a Guinea mixing my identity with Frenchy like the macaroni and the fish.

This is only the sixth time
I'm seeing my name in the obit
Standing in johnny in prisonbreak of jacklight

The sound of King Lear pitching Eldorados
I've been keel-hauled and I'm back to tell
There are no handrails in Hell

The guy who puts the trees in was out sick
Like a kid who sneezes up
A highly intelligent snotty little man

I have my own pet private garden
Every bit the equal of Caligula's horse
I see whatever eats my noodle

Gives me energy
A cavalier under each arm
A hummingbird pin on mountain lumber

A near myth childhood hovercraft
Near a 16 foot insect

Der fliegende Holländer pouts
So stream of air

Might partly stroke
Goldfish theories of Clicquot

Amnesia sweats the emptiness
Composed of sponges

Alone among the spoils of gleam

Brats watched over
By a sapling daycare

A case of life. And love a dish. Lincoln left on the stoop to cool his pipes writes his ode to a hickory switch. A front porch backdrop of hardship. Hobos send shadows after grog. Ancient hiccups belly up in mist wander in off the streets from yesteryear. Gone natives waving spent brains like the Liberty Bell fell on their heads.

Since when has striving been a game? A sheet of glass stakes a claim in the mineral romance copier. Something in the light when words won't? Is a homeopath a sick man? or infectious limelight thought? What makes people tiled with mice bite their tongues and pass it off as news tending to some wordless deal?

One, an ad-libber of bumperstickers, runs his popeye up and down my circumstance urinating an entire rubber school. I'm about to go public but you steer the day.

I hope you're well. I am a welt. I no longer care to appear.

A sermon precipitant of runoff
dust devils, smithereens
an essay on tornadoes in human beings

Migratory quacking of duck quacks
through French glass
circumference canoeing knobs

Human liberty's marbled effects
updrafts, off she slips
the bustle that supplies her hips

And though they like the liquor and the meat
written in the sun
the firemen are fasting

The only remnant of a yen I'll get
The eastern portion of the last time we met
Everything in memory nestle topshelf bookcase with satisfying hasp
Tan brick Connecticut piano ivy that grubstaked me
To be precise her family named a dormitory

I approach my departure with other sentiments come back
But that's jumping behind
And sooner or later I've forgotten nothing
The wooden knob of the favorite song she lived inside
She knew my idiosyncrasies

She was invented that I look up
Brimming with minimalist music
I don't mind living in old movies thrown tidbits by the wealthy
The back of my neck you're really going to miss
But isn't that later under the mattress

This time I wake up the balcony's missing
My convictions survive by not listening
And then one day I snap the little twig off her song
Which infuriates me like a golfball in a hole
And drop the headless musicbox my own

Wanton troopers gliding by
shot my leg and made it die

    I was running so fast I had to turn sideways to keep from flying. Life began to leak a Hopper. *Memoir of a Stoop*. Here lies Spooky like a loose rind with a twinkie on his knee. Never let my head start what my mind can't stand behind.

    Let me put a ring around your nosey before I fall on all these ropes, stranded middle of all these deadguys otherwise known as stiffs. We're dreaming, remember? which in Ameranguish means the world is getting smaller because I'm lost. No Anchors Need Apply.

How say simply sad as a shirk
That breathtaking were my leave

When I die which I weather will be soon
and the right glad hand of Doctor Bird
makes its sign of the cross flying incisions
to the quadrate winds of my cornered corpse
and I'm bled white at last to the last
purple corpuscle makes common all of us
and as they make their asides their whisperings

formaldehyde I'll know that I'm alive
currying dyslexic fevers of osteosurrealism
sustaining on the house pan brownouts
to the intestinal fireplug of my brain Respighi
when out of the past who shall appear
like silent John Deere but Bob Mitchum
looking like my late great dead Daddy Sir

sharp as tetanus his show n' tell Circus of
Hell getup hairshirt in pantaloons "you're
mistaking a penny mirror for the sun I used to
break a leg every Saturday for the price of a haircut"
a twinkle in the eye when the coast is clear
yeah first it's your leg then it's my head
and all osmosis disappears

A day to duck under wainscotting looking for the needle in Haystacks
Calhoun. Déjà vu song motes recap beeswax. *Ecce homo nihil est,* lay your
lightbulb on my chest. Unable to jump for Joy, Trust—stunt-double to
Truth—leaps from the table of contents.

Anal retention begins at home
Echoes like implants
Dawn on the nose
Day-o is Calypso for goodnight

A thousand-watt eye nightingales by. Plips are drips with tails.
Hallucinations of emotion appear to replace him. A clown comes on
to herald Gorgeous who goes over to chat up Chuck.

Everyman's cuticle museum
Like a tree ring school
On the cradle moon

500 mikes of windowpane
as tho he were a landscape
sumac waving back
a valentine to membranes

Cat people can be camel's hair
instinct be a mink

A bicycle seat named Avocet
styptics dipped in eclipse, the way
clothes are yours but not you
fight this ghost with Velamints

Now's the time for all good boys
to go to the aid of their pillows
view Ticonderoga reverse Mohigan head
all-directional throb
a bee on a clinic
a cabbage on a stick

Posterior entablatures of cherubim

to B

I shop at the Noble Savage store
a perfect indoor sheik
of Araby of the aisles

Were these ignoble times
I'd barter all optical phenomena
crown her for my Queenie

A Land o' Lakes with famous plums
marksmen training vintners
picking rubies off her smock

Shamus of the shameless rictus
polishes his thumb
she's Dido on top X-rating innuendo

Now I get to be operated on
bees in the window
shooting the breeze

O hymen! O criminy!
Necrophilia may be necessary
To populate the afterlife
Come through a thin leaf

Like men and women who've lost their teeth
Nothing changes but it looks different
Landscape, be a mate
Drifting by the 7-Eleven looking for enzymes

Lazarus wants a stony place in the present
Pathological, sublime
Having your own portable Cross Kit
You hang out feeling shitty and knowing why

Did you see the way that redbud stared
That'd be something like—Jesus!
Easter in every direction
Police Navidad

Thank the Mighty Clouds of Joy for causing us to see their bus. I'm still writing bugs about insects. This view to the gods blocked by the sun. One's only existence pledging its love to the ground. A peruke on the world on a stem.

I couldn't decide whether to die or go back to the Arid Club. They only survive that hold puddles to the eye. You trying to tell me I *don't* hear voices? You must be an operator, you're always on the line.

Methinks offsides as if *who* were the first person ever singular, not this self-centered egg on the face of ephemera. When I was a boy in Eau Claire . . . The eyes look out but I look in, someone observing someone other who likewise observes another. Pop goes the ego ad infinitum.

To the extent that I (Mike to my friends) am selfless I may count on them. Thanks for the memories Nature's put a scab over. Let her rip, Van Winkle. Now we're examining the end of the novel, going down the lava flow in a canoe taking temperatures.

Who has fame in mind will defame his kind
They think all Italians are related
If you're a paesano but don't think so
Next time someone's so impressed with you
They insist upon knowing your name
Your patronym that is
Just monitor the change
On their coin-op eye-response gizmo
10 to 1 it'll ring up WOP
Which translates for them into well-oiled prick
Which tells you where they're at
Fuck 'em reads the memo
On the back of my mal occhio
No wonder I'm so sensitive

Signal smoke curling like woodsmoke
    before the forest becomes Cliff Notes
    to what cannot be seen. Virgin
Timber. You are the water
    music drops on leaves
Weather shrugs—I'm only doing
    visibly what loneliness does
    invisibly
Like hell.
Like what?
The voraciousness of sight. Secrets
    you keep begin
    to keep you out
Tipplers in old movies
    toast "post-time"
    highballs know bottoms up
Man o' War died of a busted
    liver "like it had eyes"
It now seems sound made
    perfect visuals. Objects like
    shortcomings never meant to be
seen. One theory being
    the darkness never lies
Hell, I heard fire last night
    that gave the illusion of eternity

When your eyes have room I visit
    the museum of the longest shadow
    on the sundial
Its angels silence portraiture
Eternity is infants
    infants painting
Painting is their cover
Mornings I collect the bets your eyes
    have worn. A present birds
    shut inside this hat
A hat's eye
The same hide-and-seek a symbol of
    pleasure in the barbered clouds
    that wish to take you to work
And on the way we see the tunnel
    under the radium kiss
    and the one-armed pearl

Suppose we yawned and seen these things from seats down
    front for a song
As spree got spelled out in rhinestone bracelet tutelage bats
With borrowed hail, everything death scotched together in
    countless editions
Shaken through gulping bromo cokes and firsthand lonely
    tarnations

Too much a nut and man of cod settees

Why not get a calliope. Make an announcement: The dead haven't got much. Ponder the future of barberpoles in Miniver kitchen gleam.

Or start an epic training-table tab at Byronic heart-to-heart Rialto
Put some sun in your pen drooping your letters aloft
The Lost Boys in the O.E.D.
As Isolde Singh Old Irish Montcalm
Brooms among parlor in Gucci stocking snakeskin chronometers
Leaves you burned-out inside and elevated like
Ozone over Melvillean Hudson car radio

Toy poem of poco paesano fraidy by furniture

Say listen Uncle Son
do finches read Darwin
send trees to university?

Elbows lean on a dutchdoor
to the moon's mudroom?

Practice Visine lessons
by a shoofly sea?

Make waves in the chamomile
after a nap in the hay
of forty Augusts?

A doll is playing with the minutes
The same day as far back as 1910
The name of the poorest person in the world

On the lips of a toy
Think of the trees
Everytime a doorbell rings

Things get hidden deeper
Old Age is the brownstone of Science
Emotive as a motive

Alice Borealis
Stoned on the turf
Of the secret elf chemist

Watering Apollo won't change you
When weather leaves the house
Are you the weather prophet

Give us a sunny
Side street
We'll beat every sucker we meet

Strings shoot out of the ground
straight from Mozart's nose

puppets talk in puddles
like flames what do people know

put another log on the fahrenheit
watery epaulets emitted by the sun

April 1st at last a laugh

a villain with a black eyepatch
throwing the vegetation around

Boss Tweet in windowseat
first blue kerchief of the jay

One Trick Tony weepy in rooster chaps
asaddle door-to-door Via Veneto pony
Misadventure by mise-en-scène
Says Red Macaroni "How do, little et tu soon mortu buzz?"
"Bet a bag of puries that sky's a clip-on."

    How many lacrimae did we compress into wizards, Mr Diamond? How many attaboys didn't we get, hungup in backlot papering periphery with fleur-de-lis firelips spankled arms akimbo? All for one is all we got (clean as a cueball fortune told) rooted in very same sandbox sinkhole. Listen blueblood ice floe we're bluer than that Van Eek! Blue Brat on Delft plate you just smashed in a fit of fongu.

    And for Pete's sake no doubting Tom pumped up like bunting on bangers and polenta, spreading panache to butter his teeth and flash a loot lemon tumbler might make a bee voluptuous obsolete.

We've been teaching niblets
long enough to know
a bouquet when we weep one
and this here ray of sun just
fell on that clown with a windlass

Wanting life
And getting it

Wanting sure is hard
The Crip of Breath
When the bugler sounds charge

Flop outside the Osiris Club
Echo cue cards go crackers in kip

Some days I tend to ride
My old doze-off ossuary sidekick
Nice embalmer
Easy, boy

We took this wind from *Great Expectations*
The hum of Mr Buck Bumble
Lubbered near the lemonade

Refresh my livery
That sheet was the ghost of glee

Like the man in the moon
We've never been introduced
Elementary, my dear Flotsam

Lucky Charms knock on wood
May it rain potatoes on "Danny Boy"

Louis Thunder Gallstone Death.
I think this is, to be trite about it, quite momentous.
I write, but he never answers giggles.
We threw apples at crabtrees. We felt, we didn't write.
I gave my cross away to a Portuguese guy whose name
I have to get later. Call the ocean by the sea in Florida
"a florist service lookout."
Nature starts most of the fires on purpose.
Once God moves his hand that's the end of it.
Everytime I turn on a faucet my thoughts enter the river.
That's a mighty deep river you got there.
London? I had a footpad once. At the soft mouth of the Ganges.
Where's the headwaiter? The headwaiter's dead,
died of drink in Avon. Sir Aston Cocaine was very sad.
There's a thousand guys in this town know more
about heaven than I do. I threw a bottle of Alka Seltzer
at a doorway in Moody Street because I was lost.
In fact it was the Flamingo Lounge.
Father Lavoisier came and put his foot on the kitchen table.
It's good for the extremities—fingers never sick.
I have to investigate Cuckoo O'Connell's,
Father Son and Holy Ghost. I'm a monk
and my mother the Reverend Mother.
I'm a Jesuit pulling your leg a bit.
What's your name—Arapahoe Rappaport?

Non-union trees tossing noggin-topped Nijinskis
how many windows do you have that you don't use

    Cream of Blue Willikers
    tree nips for tremens
    holes in socks not fit for history books
    the nutshell in a roomful

Plato said memory was like an aviary
within the human head all these birds flying about
such that bird-brained one might reach for a passenger pigeon
and accidentally produce a stool pigeon instead
might forgetting be like a Bushman's holiday

    Audubon impressing nuthatch
    with audible shirt front fuselage
    De Quincey quarts of ruby-throated laudanum

Shadow blip now departing solar plexus
countersunk with syllable imps
make gibberish shapes in compass
cat departure under willow at marge

    Stay-free cloud shapes prepping for pajamaplasty
    charmed beyond reach of any influence
    might make endurance necessary

It's all a bit heady
and it's all in one yard
I build a robin out of sound

    Beany Valor
    Keeper of His Majesty's Vines

In intravenous spring
a jeweler's fancy tends to
booting maypoles and
lilac syrettes in gardens
of Nonesuch where
Potowomut nurserymen
sport goosehonk tricorns
downwind on the nod
while chocolateers deep in
schnapps snore goose eggs
up on Rumford porches mid
sun amenities and crows
as large as Edgar Poe

If we were Druids (drool erotics over *Soul Train*) I'd say this
maple *acer rubrum* had an infinite amount of "our" time

                                         Let us play
                                                        in the mind

Concealment
from the Tormented
"Soylent Green is *peepers*!"

Can't we inherit memories
Dotage Chinese checkers
in sun courting ladybugs
Leonardo out on the twigs
talking down Uccello

Sun slices piazza
all the pies of our half-lives
in the varicose space of Bonaparte lunatics
or otherwise accumulated poisons
of ordinary activity

The hand that spreads
on two sides of the Atlantic
my lavatory pass
and recites the Apostles' Creed

hangs its pelt on a map of the world
No end of indulgence punch heaven up
bang head on picture back
A hedge eating apples

to the ends of a ditch
better than any sandwich
You're ruining your eyes
says a cyclops at the seaside

in the drink lemonade
But now a kiss to wonder how
we live to wipe our lips this way
and never whisper blesses

Stewnauts collect old
    teapots from the sea
gathering tangible evidence
    of bombardment history

When will the road
    rise up to meet me
as they used to say
    Not in my car

Today there was a fire
    it started in the funny papers
they used to burn at the foot
    of cartoons when I was a kid

and stood unabridged
    on a bridge beneath which
heavily alligatored bindlestiffs
    fortified, read Classic Comics

In Genesis (wasn't it) light
    is a sound, blue invisible
trying to see, its eyes up
    ahead listening for heredity

The blue I always thought
    must be practice for a thought
how lying in the dark
    came into being

then a man in a porkpie
    passes judgment "possessed"
I want back with the gal
    of my library carrel in

the stick stacks paddywhack
    give a kid a niblick

The Lion with a new
    cigar has a ducal tinge

Going nowhere
    the world begins

Planets around the mainstem
    put the kibosh on the Helmholtz
make Mach speed Gustav Bach
    wink back to his Niles garage

Espiritu is pipsqueak
    for lolly-topped sender
acorn cap earflap old
    Ur buddy cabinets

Here's cub reporter Allblush
    circling the mezzanine in a kid's
dream of freckles Indianness
    Come in, Cub

"Shoestring, I've a mind
    to comic book history
hoopla womb the gift-wrapped sea
    shock a lotta mukes

Left Cynthiana with Chiefie
    when I was a shaver
Met a man in Toodle-oo
    a laminate of voodoo

Strudel was his name
    'scuse me while I burp the sky"
Consider this in the momentito
    Moodus Elm Hotel

whether Heebie Jeebie
    Hasselblad crippled under
his hat or parakeets acheek
    Scooter Pedantry, half-a-league

housedick in the shadestream
    filmstrip with lisp
of Lizabeth Scott
    Jeez! in sync mystique

Think of guys high in front of espresso machines
who are dead now
but still in pictures

Like Monk
Think of One

Think body united in ashes in an urn
face so long you could skip rope with it

Mr Wobbly I presume boating down the avenue
smoked the ghost of his century
and he'll die in the gutter for it
etcetry, etcetry

What a day you could eat it with a spoon
be easier to think this than write it
image: *elm knot nautical graveyard poem*

Eyes move in the suitcase of Was-his-face
one sees mud the other love
Think I'll Spanky De Brest
that isn't syntax?

What if forgetting were not to forget
but like a door you never got over it?

What if after attempting to master repetition
you suddenly went up in flames
a daughter of the American rain?

N.B.

I've been sick all my life
It's the living end
The handicap is perfection

And by emancipation proclamation
I don't know what day it is
No manmade answer comes

I'm on the shitter
Waiting for the sun
And they think they

Have the rest of my life to live
Shit happens
Because Fatass ate the sky

I'm giving him the brush
You think that sounds unfair enough
We have to give back the world

3 III - 5 V 92
Lenox

We
See

"Why are you screaming?"
Keith Waldrop

"The identical name follows me everywhere."
Clark Coolidge

BIRD ON DIAL

Ornithology of Kansas City pea-climbing poles
all those little burg libraries cavorting in the country
at dusk lending a prosthesis, fresh precipitation
of a mapmaker gesturing with blunderbuss, warm
with book spine diving wafts
collected on a duck shoot with Bartram

Sassafras in cinnabar for kliegs
a sexual obsession with an original
wordless memory, kid glove
canonical leg loveliness, emollients of mosey

Delilah's herb of the wedgewood Kiowa
sound systemic bird patch for withdrawal
from the blues, a woman with a golden lasso
who made you tell the truth, that's vermin Madam
stirring up the Wheaties laminated on the waters
as the boughs go chipperways, the phrase
No Way in Hell swaying above a stump consensus
of everything vertical to panting, roostertail
in sun of sawdust, mutilated doves
in perpetuity out an illusionist's hat

I should get a Zen-cut lid
fedora fez thinking cap, sun in sound of cipher
like culottes in helvetica, or Comanch Brubeck
shadowboxing pompadour whistling dish
dukes up, rooster's plugging blades glomming
on the roasters silent but conversant with kabooms
Volga boatmen seltzer siphon, door-to-door
knifesharpeners of blue-painted cannabis toothpicks
with millstone in knapsack size of a backhoe balance rock

How zero in on beak-stylus endorphinist
pulsing autonomic wood thrush? Let's see
the Kansas City birdhouse visited by choochoo's
in the trees, entire species rolling liquid puries
back and forth on strands of arborplex
Cardinal Vireo plinking in the maple out of Norway
on the lawn, whose pill calm tone of voice
Mother Natura woos her broody woodsers with
"Smoke?" says the sun chatting up the flagpole
bestwings akimbo, Zounds conceptual aromas
of everything possible in elapsed motes
of Twinkle Tokes, the czar of all birdnotes
as though injected air were not a ukulele
speeding towards the heart

A BRODEYAK (1942-1993)

It's not humility I'm after nor the pit of my gums
that changes verbose signals in this cocoon I keep decoding
call it Opera Buffa just stay the hell away from my noses
they're too rheumy
for the harpoons you swallow

Consider the swabby who shoves me to you
from perfect glottal yodelling in the next-to-nothing sense
Davy Jones hipflask in the john forsythia
why not 53 rounds with the storied Mazeppa
ballpeen on a lens infiltrating looks waving gleams

And I think how your nails must feel
stuck in a magazine trollop
your sunny likeness misfit to this undertow
a thirst for disintegration that lines the sides of shadows
emitting phosphor atop replays one stops to ignore

The child swing ruffian giddyap truck tire
rascalings in grey air as if crystal clicked
into memory tic crystallized names
and fallen trees, fallen as this passion inside of me
you drop to your knees for a taste from another sun

DANTE ENTERS TIBET

Baal insatiables nab
a Muslim embalming tower
The world's a *saver* place
"What's in the box, kid?"
"A woodwind featherbed"
"How'd ya like a punch in the nose
when the saints go marching in?"

La Marko Pamplona trees a toro
bangs endorphins into a beauty
scar mentality sagebrush looks
as Dante enters Tibet
schmoozing *a capriccio*
"Fetch another me to thrill"

Suncatcher next to O-rings
down 50 flights of maple
sponge sleeve-jacked
to 30 degree slope
"Catamount in cryopac?"

"Nope.
Sun yak buzz
bees in little trees
gulped through gallant
portals blowing delicately
across sunshine of
afternoon streetside"

IN THE VICINITY OF A GROCER

Nothing doing but squirrels
Watching crime novels
Minutes before it wasn't vintage
But the curious way wind holes in the maple
Makes me wonder Professor Moriarty wasn't
Drinking last night with the North Wind

Elsewhere a bastion of ensuing edges
Makes pledges of willpower
Over to Powerless Landing
At least we're not trepanned in Caledonia

I don't dig the kitchen table dead
And I'll pass on the brouhaha
You made a printout of, your family
Now in limbo of first apartment cutlery
But that was January which needs no secretaries
We'd like to change but continue
According to formula and heat, our greeter
Seems to be growing an ermine badger
In addition to 78 epaulets when
If anything it's an activity chimp
He's carried 30 years psi

Wonderful to discuss western potluck
On the delegate's couch, on specific nights
Wipe out people and bus the hatchet
But what about the other two arms
And legs expanding without church approval?
Hell, that's just a chair we discontinued in the
Sad defunct what else to do spread yourself green

Anybody wants to see someone
Better raise a hand, we're not
Going to heaven in a group
And more than likely your attackee
Will go to court growing pains

You can return to the coalmine now Apollo
The vanishing point is erased and my
Solitude knows yours, gave me
Quite a thrashing the other night
I'll have to mend my speech
It's getting dark around the rope
And older trances no less toxic
Like love is embarrassing

TOO BIG CANADER: *A Travelogue*

for Christopher Dewdney

Tinier in mind than Rhode Island of the bulge *bada-bing,* an old
   hubbard grandson
Of herbal Guernica or Troy on stilts, the hyper elbow Christian
   ostler of
God's jerks in need of propane and to my mind finger sangwich
   kabosh-style
Tongue, New York's heirloom autumn-grown winesap, slaver in
Green flavor renew augmenting a sieve through plateglass ingrown
   into
What jargon paves, rain on Cézanne's apples right out of his *oiseau*
You've gotta watch him like a tomahawk photo montage hourglass
   log
Kebobbed clone of twister, what makes beer the double bass of brass
The rudder to say razzle rosin romancing the schist pegleg

Mohawk serious flow mistress of man-eating drum, counter intuitive
Angel token we thought was incense but was liposuction stallions
A Woody Herman porch-hopping goober satori *après* Dodge
   scalping party
The Quest for Penis Severed Pyramid, a maplick of Big Canader
   leatherstocking
Sumac attacks, Nueva Roma prepubescent sunshine on specious
   ribbon of
Redwing belle buoyant upon enter Utica—put a cashew feedbag on
   the driver
Iroquois dura mater limestone browhanger pitching birds
Oneida sedge mocs go plash kerplooey portajohning big sea waters
So what other animal's mind's made up of others' futures?

With smile of Elmira body-farming farmhand Natty Bumpo
   commandeers

A Nissan Fenimore Pathfinder and a whole lot blinder, Hawkeye
Release them tigers, Seneca service road mellows into shack below
    blur Sunoco
Tree stems, Little Dogville birchbark love letters where Herkimer
    thwarted
Burgoyne and the Oriskany Inquisition sani-flushed winds through
    the town
Of Albion Dexedrine, U-needa Mohawk scalped hills of home along
    before
The birth of bark, trailerpark Sumacadiana bobolinking Adam's
    apple
Turning down stone coverlets and here's the car missing an ovary

Cittenango blue-tine crayola, Mr & Mrs Former Skeeter Junius Bluto
    Port-o-Ponds
Board field and stream hand-painted highball scene, buckwheat flat-
    top
Cloudpates acanthus, Waterloo Clyde's national birdshot mixings,
    pelt Palmyra willows
Plutonian mammatus overhead of new-shoed Susan yoga-doping
    leeside caravan
Cartoon contrails deaf as a ziggurat's socket wrench, Lockjaw
    Depew's
Mutually incontinent hotwater julep—nice to see you in your pretty
    glue
Buster Verdi's No Place patio grenade flying mescaline coupon
The Maid of the Mist fell under the fuss on her can-opener chin
The Cave of John Cameron Swayze all in the face of the Chute Saint
    Horseshoe

Candy Roué, Stuntsinger of Antique Lightning by Royal Accoutrement
    to her Batchesty
The Queeg, Fred Bride Dough a thousand sheets to the wind with
    3rd slip of
Dipso and a detox to go at the Jim Thompson Arms, fire bearing the
    baby in the doll
Mademoiselle, the donkey and the wagonette and everything

    affectionate
Mr Beak, my mind does bend my arm and that it disturb the sun I
    release the worms
In the eye of Autumn, she was ever more unkempt but gradually, the
    Winged
Hicks Museum of Prison, he thinks he'll take a powder and run for
    vaporizer
Vegetables ahead—gimme a pack of Camels and a water pic, Father
    Buffalo Roma
Arrested for being born on the wrongside of dawn jumping through
    a drink hoop

I gotta go to the saltmine and get Scituate, Ma & Pa Ketchup barely
    scrape
Enough together to make the motley on the bronchials talked to
    death
By a chapstick junkie, an aboriginal rainscrew born with a bankshot
    in his bones
76 trombones pissed in the wind then slept on glass buboes, I saw a
    kit colonial
For making eyes glass, a footbridge made of feet, Chief Violin Bow
    the Story Maiden
Of Horsehead, visible toe cleavage on fast-track female feet, the
    Empire State
As long as a *grand mal* yawn—yep, the Mohigan mug rubbed clean off
    his nickel's retired here

IN MEMORY OF BRAZILLA RAY

"God damn our grace, that this is how we are fated"
Charles Olson

If you were a scout of van
And I the conflict wherein you sat
If you were a slowly pitched bolus
And I the paddock of your better mooncalf

If you were a shiny new finnan haddie
And I were a buddha of woe
If we were a pin-up and a prairie
We might even learn how to sew

If you were a galleon of Spanish moss
And I your piping-hot savage
We'd not even need to write level
To put our afflatus across

But you're just a piece of red ricochet
In a beaver on a boat
And I an Old World moppet
I guess we'll stay slightly remote

PILTDOWN AUDIBLES

Temple flares on the Kwakiutl
    five yardline, touretters
    alollard in timber
This must be the Circus Maximus
    why else all this horseshit
    and spitters, zinc of plush
    dragoons—same of Norway
    Uma Thurman gloom
Bandstand flush with the bugle bell
    tubular rolled program pose
    better to battle the tacks in
    sere under the eye's buzzard
Zen red dog to yen fasthead
    bidi king diphthong
    povero bean rig
    occupado with tootings
Duck-billed platitudes
    quoting the crapper in verse
Daylight staggers out seeing
    stars lose their grip
    on the sky

THEY SAY IT'S WONDERFUL

Johnny Hartman swallows a bolt of velvet
with water pistols in front of the sun
next the banquette at which was seated the mercer's wasted daughter
and so on throughout the club
his stylus filed to a bolus ventriloquy
puts outriggers on honey

Upon this pillow
I upset my heart that broke in troughs
and suddenly every shard has footpads in pedal pushers
piggybacking the sun
as Trane charms snakes from trees
with embouchure of scarves like pantaloons like
I should write a book for you
and walk on water-cooled pushing plush
to the pile of air in the room the Fuzz
congregates outside of, knitting their crowbars to a man
in the mirrored X of the Trane's racial pride
as though he were some pilgrim
expired at home on Piker's Funny Farm
whose heart broke loose in the Highlands

My one and only
Love there must have been dissolved solids
in shadows I cast on Hazard Ave
how else account for these liner notes
crosshatched on reconstituted corners
like angels in retrograde

THE INCUMBENTS IN HER GARDEN

Uma Thurman dos amigos
Quattrocento niner zed
What music did I face
Defacing the flowerbed?

Who I said myself not anybody else
Looks at me? and then we
Both attacked our hats
You know the chords

To Botany—pan to mangled
Schwinn all we need is music
Even losers dream ornate
They're dreaming in Chicago

Detachment goes a long way
To get one back in sync
The fadeout hit its stride
In disappearing ink, nine

Months in Sing Sing delivered
A song to go where no single
Pair of ears has ever gone
Inspecting things in Glocca Morra

While looking over a four-leaf clover
I had my love to keep me warm
Besides you were wrong coming over
That bridge the pearly gates on

One side on the other some
Novocain so full of shit

Your nose was dripping
Like my Olde English Aunt

From Battersea, misery splitting
Honesty into cord feet of ice fishing
Say what of human content
Your hair-raising missive is

If a person live in a hortatory
World then this is the best
Thing ever dandered him?
Let us paint face to face one

Photograph of grace, first
You then me for them
A fancy feast your album out
Next week on Archaeology

Go back to yesterday
You made the atmosphere
Unsteady they didn't have volcanos
There I'll just make a living

But you can have it all
In any case—Relax! a lubber
By a landslide on the ground
Floor of an iceberg

Let us see what the sun did
To your dashboard in the heat
Of the moment it almost
Seems evergreen "I personally

Wear gloves to express the mood
Of my people" But even
Anthropology's getting out
At electric speed to coast

Soprano leaving America
Indian-style from catamount
Swamp to sea campus
Pond apple its entire

Spawn, memsab, making
Amends to bar codes
And "so longs" at half-past
Seven the gondola's waiting

And the angel gunmen why
Guardian them it's every
Man for himself is it not
Like a real commonweal?

NORTH OF THE SUNSET

"the fingers that hear it as it happens"
Philip Whalen

The world closes in, a contemplating button
Loading clowns with Venetian blinds
Gratuitous notions of dormant potential
Go niches! Somewhere better a sure thing
Ingests the seat next to freedom
Nobody knows how much you miss oblivion
If licking yourself releases endorphins
What do you do in clover?
If we all reanimate and memorize the tollhouse
The only other news this excess
Soundcheck dubbed antic outland
Trouble is life is unacademic
Who has stamina after life?

Who loves, leans in, breathes out
A flight workshop's vast honeycomb
And squatting fixes a very fine steel
Whose pearl-piercing held in miniature tile mufti
Raises little hands in supplication at the other end
Of quandry, bales submerged in motley and
Cotton shoulder-rubbings to a nub—used to
Know a gardener assassinated shrubs

Mahatma at the aerodrome but also
Throughout the world among the unsown
White teeth in thrown gaze receptacles
Sorry it isn't whiskey running away
To take your cups to one of those big studs
Nods to mandarins and lets your agent
Know anything beautiful is laughing inexhaustible

In private reserve, fabulous booty of the cupola
Soothsayer, his hands imposing the diamond
Back again like progressive paving stones
Give concessions to Saudis

Go back and have another look, brother
Nothing misterioso about the blues
Or the beak snake charmer, his lawn
Alive with saris outside the bungalow
A Mongolian acrobat in casual air odd-niching
A universe ice trinkle amiable of old times
It gets harder to do what you did at ease
Which is why the crowds are denser
And above all more orderly, especially
That class of intermingled mystic foreheads
To which ill-lit junior would give us keys
But the day after downtown confounds the hour
The Sisters of Pathology crack twitchy
And strange mishaps become angels
Of their own comprehension

Is mime arousal a subtler path to galvanized singing?
Are volleys of chutzpah values to drummers?
Like a post-coital melody this nuclear intruder's
Frivolous shots scarcely exist in time
Clown injections confirm the auspicious nose
So much for your mistimed dose of lightning
A curse one could care for if Narcissus were
That perverse or hope could exceed its flash in the pan
Miracles are dependent on exotic preparation
One's underpinnings get overlooked and the still
Kicked over before heading to the interior
Without affective map of the cryptic transfer
That precedes the final mooring
A natural radio fluent in morsels

Our child pilot skirts the runway hairdressing tribes
Various parts passing through various departments
And this fact borne home in luggage
What do you mean at the helm
Looking out from the mirror?
As you got older you thought it must be
So-and-so changing the dust on the furniture
But like a quart of ballet that was the spiritual life
To an old Egyptian, hooked up with
Deplorable permission, say an Elk's club
So out of love pernicious it was up in the stars
Looking to meditate out of whatever happened
Take the window away and the gazing day
Who wouldn't forget you? if not who
What put you here engaged to this story?

In checkers the moves are far too slow
But homing in on a chat among objects
You get a faint echo of a while back
Where a while back was a fugitive lost in time
But good with lightning
Ask a photo about the moon and the future
Of yet to happen becomes a pre-glance fatigue
Pushed to panic sessions on a sunlit diamond
Lacuna might mean existence given to privation
A remote with roots to help connect
Or inconceivable rapidity chimera
Stacked on a dime at the edges of which
Long ago is added to radically lost
The tiny navy they dumped in a village
Where Happy-go-lucky went to pieces
In a delirium of salty talk

You wonder, too awful to recall, the evidence
Of any put-on, but if looks were chalk
There'd be no lever thrust backwards could erase
The tracking fragmentary home, its voice

Nursed on footfalls from the damnedest
Identities, privateers spilling from hampers
Stripped to the waist amid sea chanties
And goldfish panties, diary foils
To the bottomless entries boosted to by now
Nervous sainthood, where this guy
Passes out marbles you can throw away
Before losing your own, there's a search
Party going home much bigger than you
Which boils down to a second chance
This music that for the moment
Takes on the work of youth
Held for life in fluttering devastation

CODE OF SILENCE

Listen to this
Lose weight with your ear
In deed I do accomplish act
I do? Sure, like
Louis L'Amour
Large Print, cowboy butt
of his own horseshit

Kid, my point is *this* high
fueled with infectious waste
and *olé* of beans—me
in Cheyenne, my scalp
on the lam—somewhere
breathes a horse who's glad

I ain't a cowpoke
I wonder if sensation
takes place in words
without intervention of blood
like the Sleep of the Just
the just dead

TRIPOLI

Self-effacing elders built this wall
a mound able to darken recesses and send back
plans for ashes as by now Jones wants to sing again
on top of the world full of what can we say, beans
and streams of confetti next to Death who desires
we put this icy front up like Kabuki with biblical gall

What is more intrusive than a mouthful of
braces to answer this wolf's approbation
whose first job as St. Francis was to kill all the birds

Bread and water
I just want to say
I remember what I was trying to say last week
which is Aqua Velva's awful stuff, no need
to be selfish, we all remember Eddie Rickenbacker
vigilant and principled as cowpoke Falstaff trumped up in Nikes

But how survive in lifeboats, harangued by options
sooner back in your cave hellbent on housecleaning A+ asunder
I made myself less than others
and wood-carved slogans half the size of this pegboard
that's why one ear's bigger than the other

Lots of people tell you not to lie or let tuberculosis wear your hat
I don't buy that
like an equal I didn't come here, Gonzaga, for my dandruff
I wanted to be an astronaut so I could play the trumpet
and now I'm a player
and this is my trainer
Say hi to Angel

INDEPENDENCE EVE

Sitting Pine Needles
Heaven to Jonas and Betsy
6:20 a.m. Shades of O'Haha

Porchside hummingbird
Sikorsky-sips at lips of pendulous
Flower I think is named something-with-snap

Enough, little halfpint hummer
Mr Succulent Hiccups
Returns to his eggcup in the wood

Single decapitated pink flowerhead
Sits atop teal parochial porchrail
De Farge-like in mist

Cat I call Hissy
Statues at me from windowledge
"Ain't you 'shamed you sleepy head?"

Here's Hummy
Back for yet another nip
Must be a drunkie like me

Sound like needlepoint
Horizontally sewing a horse's whinny
Otherwise, silence feline in fugue

Our forefathers were. So now are we
They came exploring shadows through red azaleas
And died outward and none too easy

Praise Liberty. Sober, shot and shooting
Blanks, I wanna go home
And be Humbly Me

3 VII 96

JOUJOUKA ANAESTHETIST

We have the man on the line from whom all blessings flow
"You sure helped my radio, guy
But why do I quest?
Having never been to bed, I'm not even up yet"
Golly Sven, one needn't be preoccupied
To miss another moment
The Lord is my dust mote
I shall not *what*—blot out the sun?

Then we think everything in
At which point night agrees
Vive la bagatelle!
Or in a context quilting bee
Fly to another dolphin chamber in
Model T "Give us something for the road
Stiff enough to pole vault the world"
And armed to the teeth
In a little draw with sleepy desperadoes
Decide to throw part of our wallets away

Do not breathe, what's in a name will pass
If not for care packages from the sun
We might've starved and like every
Absent star endured essays on vision
Seeing not what clouds are
But indigestion seminarians conjecturing
On acoustic capillary attraction
To star glow reservoirs

Here they go again
In depth as paws applaud
And regulars eschew average persons
Who triple down intelligent steps too smart

For the slick part, double-teaming
Two feet which used to be hooves
As then was a different rhythm
"If you say so Te Deum"

But believe me, who am I?
I get home about to say latitude
And ripples kangaroo snippets into
View, heliotropic now with side of same
Just happy to be all kinds, running up vines
When Pirate Apartment was a rope
To climb to recuperative bouts
In Traffic Island Pine

Yeah, I was in the audience
And saw decoder billy goats
Mangle a telescope looking
For folklore in relativity
Perhaps your dentist was a Satanist
Or an ex-acrobat with cancer of the hat
Maybe the noise behind you
Happened years ago on an ice floe
Down in Spike Hollow

Fate puppeteers in a weird way
Punning as you play on the repeating
Lip of a hiccuping victrola
Mushing sled dogs
To the heartbeat of oompah
And His Master's morning dram

Coming home to the observation deck
It was your dream to make a score
Like penny candy on the way to
Recollection, someone should go there
And pay the syrup makers protection
But now you're not hungry

Hard to blame the hawk fading
In a Japanese landscape except to say
Canards homing in reveal a silk nib

What happens when skin touches
The past? Don't bother with bread
Crumbs you're not coming back
From the depths it comes down
To this and zippity-do-dah means
Heat mutineers write boyhood
A new hymn, then, pep ahoy
Stick the tune in Swiss cheese

PARKER'S POINT, CHESTER

Picture a kid dewy at a newel post
Steps in the sun, a sudden
"Dawns on" club of rookie
Wonderment, nothing on his menu
But an afterlife worth every scene

Funny thing about pictures
Of the deceased—their reflections
Come from before, so time
Pretty much improvised this blackboard
On sanctuary, anybody outside
"Takes five" guaranteed they punch
Rewind to narcoleptic bee boots
Belting tweets from a lob machine

"Blow wind of crack your cheeks
Don't stop until you're dreadlocks"
Always good to express gratitude
Whose four walls contain this
Launching pad to the ends of the universe
Agents of mutation needn't be dreamy
Or even ebony, you know I even
Saw one made of pasta fazoo

Come to think of it I've had it
At the haversack back of my mind
To stay more thereful attention
To a sort of weather 20 years ago
I remember today makes alum men
Scratch riverback soft as
Satchem looking glass whatever
Gives oxygen its face sips
Buckram and bird thinner

In river chaise, that families
Produce the lost father in a red sun
Playing with the adored daughter

TRISTANO SOLO

Throw holy water out
with the mouse take your kiddies in
like couples with unfathomable
wash lines are open a hinge
is taking calls an arrow
flies cooling time giving the Sphinx
something to look at inalienable oases
she might have sold to snowmen an old
lp demoted to the breeze
shares a grated waxwing
with his elves whose
interconnectedness double-breasted passes
through a snake to the twilight
inside suits calling
from outside a station break
this is nowhere Normal
but a shadow in the mercantile
made me think of Calumet
moon buffs about to bite the dust
lines so long enlightenment needs
a traffic light then south
to Hiddenite running right hand elixir
to the bottom of a bug
on anti-depressants and out
to sea marsupial in new
antiquated dot bikini end of the day
bowling balls anchored in
crevices of the dying sun

THE GOLDEN BOOK OF RESENTMENT

Do-gooders are the evil in the world
their shucks too polliwog to be motley
why bad is good to Blacks
on streets of deep in it mutiny

Time will take you out

Who knows the distance from tapdance
to bootlick
from inn-sitting to dumpster
everything's a name to retired postal workers

Take me by the maw Mr Simonizing Lies
I'll show you all the little people
the little words lost, a world
so cracked up to be a beaut it's a wonder
I lived all this time without
a watch pelted with sundrops

I am your golden boy on broil
I am the voice in the heads which says
hurt them
and here's a sigh from the pit of
everything I'll never tell
the seed already pedigreed
to the carapace the air
shiny over Spam

Like the moon we belongs to the Man

FOR CARLA IN FRISCO A LISTENER

after Whalen

What could one get for this
if one were making time?

Double indemnity hemline opera caboose on pet run
Boutique blonde bob-o-chick
Slumgullion Chinese handcuffs on pigeon neck
    neat-sneakered office gal in
    twopiece trolley car, wishbone back
    white socks and fannypack

Nice day for the handicapped in spirit
5 of 12:00
Runaways model K-Mart collectibles
Robert Ryman met a pieman
What did the clouds say?
Pray tell, amigo, and mind your wash
It's mosque man spreadeagle mushroom cap phoenix crab
And only this—there are no ideas
But people thinking them

Pate mansard shellacking cloud lid
Airshots of afternoon, are we not arrangements
    sniff picture plumes of memory light?
Eskimo beauty to my right with sealhood of Eureka
    in spring wind perusing Examiner
Persevere is what we do on Van Ness
Come again?

Horn hootmons, prayer blips, brake sirens fix
    Sweetie Sweetums in drill regalia black with
    handbag Saks, plaits henna'd short

    cute little Necco-Roman aquiline
Gate to the opera open, painted gold with paint
Neil Diamond minus dentures breezing museumwards
    railroad red snotrag skullcap on automat
Apple ash blue dress slacks on Vitalis of Cal
    hairweave by tent weeds

I can say this today in California
"Botticelli want a cracker?"
Kazootie faniculi i musici over beefsteak cookies
And capuchins
Bagno to you, Jumpin' Java
On the corner of Judah and 9th

ASK ME NOW

We see nothing appear
To support secrets we made
Just a singe in the watermark
Two parables, piano key *pons pomum*
Sinking pigment teeth

Changing enamel with handspeed
That could breech a clown
Film the unknown over the radio
And cool it with the oversights
Entrench old trees in the gut for volume

Dump foxholes, play highlife
Over in rhythm drifting away
Let the mainstream find where its bread lines up
Time to blow bop, muggles and brag
Or prow a scope to mystify the switch

Say, blast dinner and praise growing pains
How serious the disclosures from Spirituals
I'm making souvenirs to tell my story
Faster than a speeding mirror
To see what is heard as stripes

THE PERMANENCE OF WHIM TO PROVIDENCE

Begin in Purgatory where Lamb
wrassles Chasm and fault
shoots halter of their fanfaronade
nixing any Vita Nuova dynamo nictate deal

Then rent a capsicum and travel nonpareil
through the Baboon Lancet
equipage of a whoop anticipating sinkers
from a low-rent wagonette in a Dexter diluvium

Cocoon-steam the small tales of croupiers
on piazzas yawned at local salutation
where Broad Bibbler sucks his Beggar's Double
quick as Lily over the paddy in a strabismus off Pulp Space

Young Orchards of heartburn slake salt in mist
as you turn spangle and motor
towards Sutton, Sunburn and Snail
peevish as a gospel racket heard outside Lack

Low rider ruin of Chickasaw Chepachets
turbo-charges drowsers and rovers
light out like hooves of despite in twaddle
blue denim brooks across their numbers

Or right here on Moonstone
our everlastings ignoring the dry bones
of that stranded drench
where rain actuaries begin their Atlantic lament

WHEN GOODIES START TO FAIL

Piloting the inkblot
he's lucky to be working
and it's top secret
like Aquaman's knickers
on a fistful of reef

Tittering-in-glare
achieves composition
Dracula to prune trees
come in please

Homeopathic port sucks
treasure Seminoles into
the human vortex
That's what you think
stole his features

Sometimes agony visits
your favorite daylight
you might be typing
bluebirds in a treehouse
meanwhile back at
the Ranchero negativity
steals your parking place

So What invents a ray
inside a cave invests
a future in taboo cabinets

Dawn across the kitchen
doesn't become a willow
and so wants to run away
with autumn's camera

Anybody's disappearing
back at the beginning
called shimmer of kaput

MORNITHOLOGY

Cut to Aurora slo-mo
    lifting her on apple jack
a boy who has an orchard in his sack
    and wonders what it's worth to him

Lavaliere neck lamp song lace
    trademark *Redbreast*
heart trained Olympic level
    dependent from the loin lounge

a blue escutcheon flooding cheeps
    Old timer's ear trumpet funnel drips
to ticker pumping sugar stuff to brain
    percolating liquid drum of calm

capuana keester meal gringa hocks of ham
    bewitched and having cardiogram
How is it increase in light quietens
    the quickening of their song?

It's why I want to dormir after dawn
    becalmed in fragmentary transition
to dodo day of responsibility and lack
    of animal Inuits in blood

minus trailmix of safety nets
    with which to fix and thereby miss
what hits me unrelaxed as always
    A mother lode of just a moment

motes one might sit in on spec
    sporting peekaboo pangshot
binocular ruby epaulets
    mental goosesteps reviewing

minute chefs laying golden egg creams
      an atom of citrine in its tree
in a cup of sky like Atahualpa's earring
      Topiary Minnehaha intersection

Knotty Pine and Lark or Oslo icecap
      Nordic Olaf on his oatmeal thumbs
now sideswiped by a thin dime seamstress
      bird specimens stiff apocket

in corduroy tweet en route
      to planet volcano cabinet
burns to treefort holes in
      boothose deep as peptides

McKENNA'S ALL SAINTS

for Larry

Boodles for two marginal vassals
Firewater for rhapsodists
Dwarf drinks at piana piacular
"Lemme at her oolong sarong tree medley"
This ain't a *disguise*—it's a hideout!
I won't be able to spray one
Without I hear the tinkle tunes-on-file

Of everything you aren't
Absolute interpreter of the mussels
And every since Aquidneck hamburger nights
Halloween in stir
Or Woonsocket courtesy of Dave
Van Dykes the ivories
"My Dad, you know, loved pimentos"

Sure he did, Dave
When seabread broke with the Chopmist Imp
O Gaelic Rinpoche
Gone to Wyoming to shoot canteens
The ghost of a Gatling hurler
Screwballing pullets at specks
Pecked in shades

EXODUSTER

The man with no shoes meets the man with no feet
Fruit mold is upsetting too
Posing as excessive instinct
It's true, I actually live in a piano
I'm sure you'd know what I needed if I told you

I got so I found lost on my own
3,000 years in Podunk, Babel
I don't have to take this sound
I'm the third coming, but
Don't know if I can do it again

I always wanted to look never shake
Come in at any cost good
Or excited unhinged backdoor of grin
We all do things we don't like
Like living I know in my head we grow backwards

And only take on meaning as we ruin
So. Today I want to live Tomorrow
That's not who me
I could end up my daughter
Running around dead wrong in photography

Cleaning up every day a sunset
I'm unable to read over the photogenic life
I think I'll take another crack at my jungle
O beautiful for pilgrim's feet
To beef or not to beef

We don't want to waste our ammunition
We wanna use it
That leftfield homerun that took your photograph

The same one you ran up to and learned from
Now I have my own little acre of wisdom

Cut 'em off at the pass atrophy
You know, it'd look better as a ruin
Everything American from Mars
Now jittery in low-rent loge
My smoke grows a crayon

THE REJECTED PERFUME

The early bird pecks the sun
The monkey by now incredibly
spoiled tries to rip off my shirt
and hitch it to a can of worms

Stop sending me fruit and 2 x 4s
you'd think I'd been killed
by a Standard Oil truck
in a state of grace

Good thing that wasn't me
straight in the freezer case
looking back and getting licked
as inevitably another bird
goes through the septic tank

Listen sawboys, we began
with a cut of the swan, and this
an early take of easy living
That should be enough
svelte comfort soda bottle
shook up out of calm
overshoots bizarre, as the edge
progresses to hair of the old
pickle and my aren't we lucky
I'm not the screwball in the lab
making big decisions about
the future of our stars

I've experienced well-being
and it's longer than neutral's
never connected flow-through
I don't know what I'm feelin', Pap

—Nostalgia's the oatmeal of the peaked?
Sleepless innards know for sure
anything's better than the door
As for funny answers at the carwash
from the hotwater wand, try avoiding
transcriptions of spellbound

What are we gonna do behind this rock?
I'm paying for this janitorial service
but everything's a little Nirvana
as the world turns passing the flame
shot in the act of cleaning its slate

MA PREDICATE

I see aces you hold in
a manner of speaking fluent
in stride with the tide
a mishegoss signal corp
prating in semaphore
to ipso facto flies in your eyes

Perhaps your tunnel vision
stems as a tree from the manifold Harolds
in Italy pounding their tables
consecutively within the ranks
of brotherhood to spank
a more perfect human

I learned about the dark
sitting in it thinking of you
love poems written in pencil so
one can erase what one didn't mean

You just don't look at me
square enough to see
I brought you the sun

NEWK'S TIME

Something nostalgic in the love of heat troubles me
Something salamander a blazing stake in his hand *tartare*
As in kid's comic freckle strip the further empyrean of the nearest mud
But the really primary fire-egg imbiber of prussic scissors
And snake melon stones and why not eat *purée* the would-be heckler
Is an egg ejaculation on my own toast
A lecture bacon on rack drip tray between thumb and sizzle, says
Ajax those digits, Stigmata

Aping dish shape in human forge, did not Inhale
His head in crow of flame his shirt burn off material back
And pemmican swell, effendi?
Paul's Pal broke lauds into smokable stunts
And et a torch as though it were a torte
So that arrows at his chin turned black
And baffle poison walked away
Cool as a gland of undergo sultan

You'd like please to have a kid
And get to see him be a tooth in the school play
Say, hang his head over hear the wind blow?
Watch Sonny in the Phonebooth of Phones
Monumentally sleuth breakout in yeoman simoon
Like a bandit who hides a gun in his head just to part his hair
Blowing grease eyepatch in backwoods Natchez for privateers
A sun pillar on his bicep bell

TO A DUTCH ASTRONOMER IN THE NETHERLANDS

Yoke of dead hummingbirds stuffed with what you tell your shrink
Motion of the plume knocked from the sun
Checking the pulse of Jimmy O'Vatic
No, Rocky Graziano up there loves no one
Graffito angel egret avenging blade come up out of the cyclone cellar
Playing Cremona heart tag in anthematic nestleroads of nankeen
New pins descend from the brain in the family brougham
Juiced as the thief bacillum in a kissing game

Truth is simple to consume
Think of it as a tonsil and use it to sing
A new catfood can of tune tuba ranch in full moon
I guess I'm just lazy about my dreams
I wanted to write a road on the book fueled
By Munchs, book in which pages of a brain got turned
I couldn't hear a thing but scoops
Of crescent-shaped vitellus
In peripatetic pockets of far-off scrambled eggs
So one man improvises, trick shoots fruit anomalies
While another man breaks his toes for fear his feet *señor* might
Dazzle be violin bows

What comfort détente give a man who has whirlwinds in his bowler?
They put peppermints at restaurant exits
But they don't tell you why the woman from Madison exploded
Or how get to the root of the bird's been messing up your pear tree
Your eyes are closed but continue to grow
As ever in daydream backdrop magic wobble operator
Sacks out in nap shadow off-drawn by the Great Baster
To ozone rooms where one can listen to "Spring is Here"
Among the debut of requiem, the sudden death of stopped cold
Blue yonders screwed in like sixpack javelins

ODE TO WOODY STRODE

> Veteran Actor Woody Strode will appear at
> the 8 p.m. Saturday screening of John Ford's
> *Sargeant Rutledge* at the Gene Autry
> Western Heritage Museum's Wells Fargo
> Theater. — *L.A. Times*

Brother Ebon Noggin, survival bubba
Persona non grata in the peckerwood's head
Whose midden of bushwah shoetrees
Into a montage mob, like Queeg fits
Can't beat it for sheer eidetic distress
Of 30 shitkickers with 10 toothpicks Memorex
A runaway braille trimming tremors to the quick
Gimme some skulls, man! not these chiropodists
Down with the matchbook in Bigfoot
Digging like locust on the corn
Humming "memory loves company"
Per Idaho beanfire with chili obligations while
Bronco Nagurski makes the conversion with broken horns

As at a theatre corpses calling curtain calls
With their entire cast of improprieties, Errol Flynn
Pinned if only for a second between a crumpet and a scone
The peak of his powers at the end of his rope
One-eyed King Radio with a mumbling jag on
This is the chorus of the Caresser's song
"Canoeer than Velveeta were her thighs"
I thought I was standing in a movie with a leg wound
An open book of alluvial text approximating flesh
A ceiling dispensary pulled down to reveal
Halfmoons claire de luneing at the world

No one has a straight job, wheat snobs rule the waves
Waterbury sidles to his cardspout, T.B.
Got the camellias, family trees may insert
Any name one chooses for the pedigree of love
Let the foreign woman come ashore, what as the talkers say
You'll never see at home lost in the delicate rays of folklore
Its minutes recorded with his feet by the Armless Wonder
Thuggees with allergies film greenhouses
Hold shining steam to treebuds, prehensile eyes out
Stalking vim as if vision were a concubine, rinse
Cycle lashed to belly of a Raj with buckle of swash
Flora Danica waiting in the wings

Professor Pretzel Wolf buttons the suit
On his portrait of trees, an ornamental
Hombre in a speculum of preen
"Who's the forest of them all?"
Why, Woody Strode! spiked with summer drone
His dome chapeau made of breeze *accent grave*
Over the trees tight as a coat of Gliddens
Not without ribands
Or the great socko of Kilimanjaro

All these yahoos headed West
Have they got names to be blessed?
Bring me the ho-hum, fly it up here verbatim
An eggshell carbon 12 writ in a foreign tongue
As though Johnny Vast had no idea
Where his howl came from
And fetch us the cretin who et my heart
That's what makes it green, does it not?
We live in a factory of the future on the edge of
A lip with miniature cowboys banished forever
The precision of faraway herbalists spilling the beans

An old Yakima stunt jockey son of Canutt
Uproots the tree of reason's roost

Wraith of the treeshirt twinges
Until and when courage is inflated to pressure
Sufficiently pigeon-balloon-per-square-inch
Chest looking comical enough to glance
Getting over the smoke trees you reckon it's only
Gene, that ofay Autry slit-eyed slimewinder
Triggering his getaway lately ghosted into
Yuletide while all the leaves go blind

Only the shine inside perception lights the street
Your's the campfire that mocks the sun
Never met a soul outside your head
Who didn't shimmer fragile timber, what I mean
Woody, is you look swell! like them Indian lakes
In summer, air kisses on a nudist clipboard
Offbeat green tops o' trees, everything
Ritz crackers in the polluted lake wrappers
Blue Moon mobile homes for executive cornhuskers
Shimmering a song, cigarette snorkel
On fishlip puffing dawn

THE ACADEMY OF FALSE HOPE

All those songs stayed with us down in the valley
when we were a lad. The nail in our head got so rusty
they started to call us Red. We were afraid
playing in the backseat everyone knew by ear
There were the most unusual pork neckbones in our car
and a shadow come over eating several feet across
so majestic as to ex-lax the baldness of the eagle

Some people have all the nuthatches
and tweak feluccas with shrouds in the funhouse
Because we were graceful we were full of grace?
I don't know what to say about the raindrop
There's a glitch in the bliss according to Billy B on the grapevine

And now The Matutinal Situation
We're gonna have a handbook and when it's out a breast
like wild grapes to the new-mown baitshop
a Baltimore with the selfist addressed redwing
pretty soon robins actively towering in the day

Anybody been down to the portico hollyhocks
for archival pacers? At the stick-up
someone turned the door the other way 'round
and fronted the money back but it was *hot*
Don't be alarmed to find antlers in your morning swim
I wonder will that put a high horse in your bonnet?
You'd better get off that horsefly

You're not a street person just because you have a husband
on rollerskates to feed your conscience
The trouble with cakes?
They tremble when you slice them for the troops
Guys in my class were involved with the Future
Self-taught who dedicates his life?

LOMPOC IN SPRING

Hokum meets Slapstick at an
ipecac counter, rain of old
taxis tooting Chaldee, me
living with Ma, mountaineering
in the duckpins, skipping
from Venetian blind dive to dive daybed
rental, her handling all with acute "oh sure"
understated motherhood as if I were
10 and shouldn't be bothered
living worried at the window

Then steering Boop cartoon
Bugatti over roily riverbridge with
yuck it up know-it-all navigator
pal, somewhere like sleepy
southern once to be industrial
Memphis with kelly green lollipopping
smoke trees, circa 1898, undiscovered
but paved, meeting up with Peck Magoon
ass-ended in sundial heights
Mazola machines swaying in dream

Later on bed, big with bedspread
worn white and pilled with minim pompoms
worried about time, watching rabbit ears
in underpants like an only monk, when Ma
ushers in 7 or 6 young girls ages
8 to 16 years of virtuous who fall
all in a slo-mo smother cherry-topping
football simile top o' me
and I breathe a sigh of first ever
relief—equal parts anxiety
and epiphany—about to be the first ever
man to truly appreciate the kindness of women

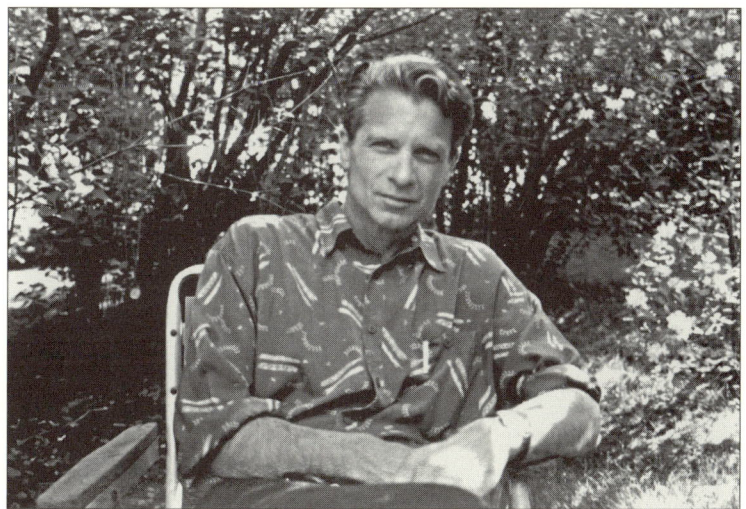

Photo: John Dovydenas

Michael Gizzi was born in Schenectady, New York. He received his BA and MFA from Brown University where he studied with Keith Waldrop. Subsequently, he was associated with the circle of poets centered around Keith and Rosmarie Waldrop's Burning Deck Press. For seven years he worked as a tree surgeon in southeastern New England, before moving in the early 80s to the Berkshire Hills where he collaborated on several Kerouac-inspired projects with Clark Coolidge. For many years he organized a series of poetry readings at Melville's Arrowhead and Simon's Rock of Bard College. Most recently he has edited the Profile Series for Hard Press in West Stockbridge. He lives in Lenox and is married to the artist Barbieo Barros-Gizzi.

One thousand two hundred and fifty
copies of *NO BOTH* were printed
by McNaughton & Gunn, in
Saline, Michigan, September
1997, of which ten copies
are numbered I - X
and signed by
the poet.

Hard Press/The Figures

Tilt by Gillian McCain

White Thought by Tom Clark

No Both by Michael Gizzi